WITHOUT FEAR

Also by Michelle Young
Salt & Light

WITHOUT FEAR

Michelle Young

Without Fear

Written and arranged by: Michelle Young
Cover Art by: Mitch Green at radpresspublishing
Edited by: Catherine Milos

Learning to build a better boat
    –   Kenny Chesney

DEDICATION

To my beautiful daughter: never change. Please don't ever let anyone, including me, especially me, tame your beautiful wild spirit. Remember you are wanted, you are loved and you are perfect just the way you are. I love you, always.

AKNOWLEDGMENTS

To all the readers, the poetry lovers, the survivors: you are the strong ones, the courageous ones. You inspire me every day to keep fighting and to never stop writing. I hope you can learn to transform your pain into something beautiful and grow from it.

I'd like to thank my family for their support, patience and advice during the review and editing process of this book.

Thank you to Mitch Green at radpresspublishing for your talented hand at creating the cover design.

A big thank you to Catherine Milos for your detailed edits and suggestions for this book, I'm so grateful for your time on this.

To my sister, Karine Landry, thank you for your incredible support and love through this process.

I also want to say a special thank you to my husband, John, for your continuous and unwavering faith in me and my writing, as well as your encouragement and advice along the way.

Lastly, thank you to my beautiful daughter, Melissa, for being the inspiration for this book with your fearless bravery and unyielding determination. I love you.

NOTE TO THE READER

Without Fear is a book about pain and healing. The words in this book express both vulnerability and strength. *Without Fear* is not divided into different sections like my first poetry book *Salt & Light*. Instead of sections marking the different stages in my journey towards healing, this compilation is one body.

In my experience, pain and healing come in waves. The ups and downs happen throughout life and cannot be compartmentalized; they often occur simultaneously and without warning.

It is my hope that, as you read this, you allow yourself to feel vulnerable, while acknowledging the strength growing inside of you.

WITHOUT FEAR

Michelle Young

Her pain is marked upon her skin.
In open wounds and scars
she planted seeds and watered them.
Tears turned brokenness and pain
into a beautiful garden.

The queen had lost her crown
thinking she'd find it at the king's feet.
Glimmering on the ground, she picked it up,
feeling the heavy weight of it in her hands.
She wiped off the dust and realized
a crown is just a crown —
she doesn't need one to rule.
She placed the crown on a shelf.
What's inside her is much better.

Some nights, I lay awake,
afraid of the dark.
Frozen in place —
terrified by my mind.
All my worst thoughts
take up space,
when I need rest
to fight against them.

She lost her wild.
"Be still", nature whispered. "It will find you."

Expectations have let her down,
dropped her to the ground,
and broke her.
Until she stopped expecting
anything at all,
and life surprised her.

She sat by herself in the room —
mending her wounds as best she could.
Her candle lighting a small space
she felt lonely, but safe.
When other candles began burning around her,
she saw she was not alone in the room —
others were healing from the same wounds.

A hatchet cuts chunks out of a tree trunk.
Your words chip away pieces of my soul.

We can't blame our nose
for running and catching a cold.
We can't blame our head
when it's hurting and darkening our soul.

Take me to the mountain,
I will get high at its peak and
be cleansed at its foot.

She cuts the silence with her screams —
bruising limbs to be heard.
She doesn't have the words, only strength
for others to see and hear
her worst pain and fear.

I refused to remember you as you are now.
All the hope I clutched to vanished into thin air.

Unfortunately, I will always be searching and starving. The food that sustains me doesn't exist in this life.

For years, I didn't bother looking at my reflection.
I don't wear make-up, so I figured it didn't matter.
But every day I ended up looking right into a mirror,
those little eyes copying my behaviour.

How can you ignore my existence for so long, then get mad when you reconnect and I've moved on?

I've fallen deep into the ocean,
seasick by all the turbulence.
My vessel no longer keeps me safe.
To remain in it would make me drown.
Rust and holes make up the floor I'm standing on.
An anchor preventing me from reaching the shore.
I can see it on the horizon
but I don't want to leave my broken ship behind.
Even if it means sinking to the bottom with it.

Standing still is too ordinary for her.

I've seen more disturbing and terrifying things
inside my own head
than out there in the real world.

Chase after the light.
Jump over the cracks in the ground
that want to swallow you.
Cling to others who shine bright,
and hope some of it rubs off on you.
When you can't see the light anymore,
create it yourself.

He made a home inside of me,
crawling beneath my skin,
I tried to push him out,
but too much time had passed.
Even though he's long gone,
he's still part of my DNA,
still has a home inside of me,
and I've lost the key.

I live on a highway between obligation and freedom.
Somewhere in the middle, I find my salvation.

Wasting time has the same consequences
as investing money poorly.
It costs us a lot and we can't get a good return on it.

When everyone else saw black poison in my veins,
you found splinters in my heart,
helped me pull them out
until my blood ran clear of my past.

So bad at allowing myself to be happy.
I sabotage every opportunity before me.
I've become my own worst enemy.

She fell to the ground
and dust covered her.
The wrong one saw only dirt and left her there.
The right one saw the beautiful creature she was,
blew off the dust, and let her rise again.

I am an angry, forgetful, and rude person who points out everyone's flaws, doesn't show up, and ignores your texts. I'm also a hurt little girl with self-esteem issues, who sleeps all day and feels disappointed and scared all the time. Yet you never notice that little girl because my words are so mean and my actions are so loud. You can't see my loneliness and sadness. You don't notice the silence.

She came running to me —
her little finger bleeding.
"It hurts mommy, take the pain away."
I kissed it better and wrapped it in a bandage.
"All better. Time will heal it," I told her.
Later, she saw me sitting on the floor
with my head in my hands.
"It hurts, baby. I can't make it better."
She kissed it better and stuck on a bandage.
"All better. Time will heal it," she told me.
If only kisses and bandages could heal the thoughts too.

I wanted to die.
To escape,
to be free,
to rest for a while.
But the thoughts follow me.
They will find me, even in death.
Unless I deal with them in life,
they will follow me until my soul turns black.

It's so natural for me to be afraid.
It's almost comforting for me to be scared.
I can't get off the ledge.
I'm terrified of what's behind me
but even more of what's ahead.

I'm not tired. I'm just empty.

She trusted his words,
but ignored his actions.

"Take it off! Make the pain stop," she says.
I wish I could.
I'd take all the cuts and bruises,
cover my skin in scars,
just to leave yours perfect once more.

I wanted to save you, all of you.
I saw myself in your eyes
but I couldn't control your mind.
You didn't want to be saved.

Crushed by the weight, unable to breathe.
You sucked the life right out of me.

A small drop of faith makes the enemy tremble in fear.

Run towards your life so fast
that your shadow is left in the dust.

In the city, I feel distant from myself.
The bright lights, the rushing cars —
they make me breathe faster, not deeper.
When I drive towards the water,
the forest or the mountains,
I feel peace again.

She's a wild ember
flying in a stormy night
with no destination.

Rainbows, a symbol of hope.
Colour, when all I could see was black and white.
Your way and my way:
never an alternative, never an option, never a discussion.

Insomnia has killed my brain cells
and devoured my memories.
I'm only a ghost of who I used to be.

Your threats kept me from speaking up years ago,
but they aren't working anymore — are they?

She never thought she'd find herself in someone else.
But when she saw those kind eyes,
she knew she'd found a home.

If what you love to do has no purpose at all,
do it because it makes you smile.
That is reason enough.

I still taste you in my words,
when the poison drips from my lips.
You were always the darkest side of me.
When all I wanted was mystery,
you gave misery.
When I wanted happiness,
you gave sadness.
A game of opposites.
Called me close, then attacked.
My soul for a kiss.
Played a game with the devil, and lost.
Spent a lifetime trying to find my way home.
You left me on a deserted street
with only the clothes on my back.
Having to learn again how to walk with my own feet.
Remembered who I used to be,
before you decided for me.

She is a complicated shadow of who she used to be.

She was drowning in depression,
choking on breaths of anxiety.

She's a beautiful mess of chaos and strength.

I want to be yours — intertwined, never apart.
Melt together. Become one.
Where I don't know who I am, without you in my heart.

Love her wildness.
If you are brave enough for the task,
she will fiercely love you back.

Your love is as gentle as rain,
but as solid as ice.
The wind won't carry it away.

I was buried alive under layers of mud
and crawled out alone.
Yet, the dirt left on my face
makes you uncomfortable.

Helping others is wonderful,
but you need to save yourself first,
or do no helping at all.

She's a leader with a presence;
an example of courage;
a heart of gold that lives in the moment.

Feel the pain that buries you underground.
Cry over what hurt you.
And, one day,
you'll see it transformed.

My demons have names.
There one minute, gone the next.
Never far enough, but just out of sight.
Appearing at my weakest, and at my strongest.
Using every opportunity to take bites out of me.
Making sure they keep their mark on me.
Never letting me believe I'm good enough —
reminding me I'll never be free.

Don't be tamed by the thoughts in your head.

The coals are still hot
days after the fire has burnt out.
The words still sting
long after they've left your mouth.

When we met, our demons shook hands, and made plans.
Assembled weapons and rallied forces.
We were the soldiers of choice,
the ones who would do the fighting in their place.
Placing one against the other,
we never knew we were on the same team,
fighting the same demons.

She taught me more about myself in one year
than in all my years.
She just copied me, and I knew what I needed to change.

Tiny fingers make tiny ripples that become crashing waves.

I wish I could forget all the good times.
It would make it easier to hate you.

Air so thick,
lungs too small.
Chew it up in small bites,
always hungry for survival.
A struggle to keep breathing.

I sleep at the base of the mountains,
where the waves crash down.

Your bank account doesn't impress me,
your passion does.

I can still see clearly,
all the little details.
I could draw from memory:
the lines around your eyes,
the shape of your hands.
It might not be that easy
to erase you from my mind.

She chooses to make friends everywhere she goes, without bothering to learn their flaws.

Mental illness is an invisible sickness.
It blackens the soul,
and creates terrifying thoughts.

Our toothbrushes kissing in the glass
were more intimate than we were.

Demons haunting us in the night.
Walk in my dreams
like they were invited to the party.
They don't seem to notice the silence around them
when they settle in — make themselves at home.
They don't see they're not welcome anymore.

He was already claiming what he thought was his before she realized she needed to start labelling herself.

Over time my eyes adjusted to the dark.
I'd forgotten.
I was searching for the light.

I don't know how to fight well.
I will not stop slicing you open with my words,
so desperate to get a reaction from you.
Like trying to burn an ice cube.

Pulled her close like a whisper,
only to scream inside of her head forever.

We are small in between the trees,
but tall amongst the grass.
Our perspective on our situation
can change everything.

She shouts at the wind like wolves howl at the moon —
in complete abandon.
She trusts her voice will be carried through the night.

I prayed for strength.
God sent me a daughter.

Snow makes everything look magical in a season when most things die.

On the nights where the enemy hallows me out
like a pumpkin at Halloween,
God uses the emptiness
and fills it with light.
So that I may brighten the path
for others walking my way.

I fell off the mountain into a deep valley
where I built my house,
forgetting completely
about the mountain where I came from.

I like you more now that you're silent,
never having to pay attention
to the pauses between the words.

Never again will I trade my voice
for a promise.
Never again will I sell it
like cheap jewelry.
It took me years to track it down —
I gave up much to find it.
Now that I have reclaimed it,
I won't ever give it up again.

Head pounding, neck sore.
I can't hold the weight anymore.
I have to unclench my hands,
let my anger fly away,
and hope to feel lighter day by day.

I need the rain so I can sleep,
but the rain doesn't need me for anything.

She played dead
when she should have let her voice be heard.
She'd never heard of his kind of beast before.

My pain is so strong
it thunders throughout my entire body.
Hugging myself tightly,
trying my best not to tip over
each time it roars.

My demons look for you each night,
but my angels blind their path.

A laugh is better than a thousand kisses.

I'll always be surprised by
how much you love me.
How you love the darkest parts of my soul,
when I'm too arrogant to do the same.
Even after all the hurtful things I've said,
you stayed.
Whether because of love or loyalty,
maybe simply a deep hope for me,
to return to the spark of light
you once saw shine within me?

We hide our vulnerable selves from our friends
out of fear of exposing just a little too much
of our true selves for them to tear down.

She has made me my ugliest
and my most beautiful self.
She has shown me all my levels of patience
and my lack of.
Her gestures have broken my heart
and grown it.
She's learning from me,
but she's also teaching me.
She looks up to me,
but I don't want to look down at her.
She's smarter than I realize,
kinder than I expect,
and more resourceful than I give her credit for.
She's got an adventurous heart,
a courageous soul, and a joy for life.

Potholes to a child are just puddles to jump into on rainy days.

Waves crash over me, relentless.
I can't breathe. I can't catch a break as they hit.
The tide is up and I'm falling deeper and deeper.
The storm above rages on, muting my screams for help.

Scars are white.
Ink is black.
Tell me, would you prefer actions or words
when I fight back?

We buy blackout curtains and tint the windows of our
cars.
We have light switch dimmers and air conditioning.
We spend too much time indoors in the summer.
We keep trying to block out the light
while looking for the meaning of life.
We keep finding shelter in the shadows when it's not safe
there.

My mind never lets go,
no matter how tired I am.
I learned long ago
how to detach my mind from my body.
It used to help me survive,
taking my mind to a faraway place,
but that faraway place never stops.
I've visited so often
that I don't know how to come back to the present
and be in tune with myself.

Wild hair and muddy feet. Grinning from ear to ear.

Face as delicate as a flower. A soul as loud as a lion.

I'm finally an adult:
no longer afraid of eating alone;
won't hesitate to open a bottle of wine on a Tuesday
night;
I pay all my bills on time;
and I learned to say no.

It's hard to explain how much I crave your touch.
I usually try to express it by hurting you.
No wonder you get confused.

I'm so mad that you know so much about me,
but, mostly,
I'm disappointed I showed you so much of myself.
I should have kept some cards closer to my chest.

Find your tribe.
Not those who want to change who you are,
but those who embrace who you are.
It's not just about bonding, it's also about surviving.

I lie about how I am
and now I've forgotten who I am.

Being numb is a familiar place for me.
It's often too late when I realize there was a fire burning
inside me.

I may as well set the table for three
because depression comes each night hungry.
I may as well add a pillow and make room for all of us
because anxiety likes to lay between us.

He still exists even though he's gone.
My mind keeps him alive, haunting.

My biggest regret was that I never told anyone the truth. It might have helped all the others after me.

Water droplets in the sun sparkle.
Tears can shine like diamonds.
Our pain can be beautiful.

Stay with the one that keeps you smiling
long after you've hung up the phone.

He's no longer the one hurting me.
He trained me well enough to do it on my own.

Their looks, most disapproving,
looking in at our struggles,
never offering help,
but offering judgement instead.

I gave up.
I hit rock bottom.
When I finally got up, I realized
I was standing on solid ground.

He never had her from the start.
She was already scarred by her past.

Nail marks in my palms —
crescent moons of dried blood
from when I held on
when I should have let go.

He has a name,
this fear that lives inside me.
I know his face,
he haunts me daily.
I close my eyes trying to block him out.
He whispers doubts in my ears.
He won't leave me alone.
He must break me completely,
snuff out all the light,
until not one ember is left behind.
So that we are forever tethered together
and I can never be free again.

I hate my mind, but amazed by it.
Sometimes, all I see are terrible things —
demons and fears clawing at me.
Other times, I only see good —
hope and love warming me.

He searched for her sitting in the shade of the sun.
She was dancing in the moonlight.

The angry bull comes knocking at my door.
I've led him straight to us.
He comes in and begins destroying,
breaking everything and scaring us.
Out of the house, we go running
and he chases after us.
It doesn't matter where we go hiding.
He'll always come for us.

Uprooted from place to place;
constantly on the move,
never having a place to call yours.

Is it the fact that you're still alive
or that you were born at all
that strengthens your faith in God?

I love the way you can see the tall mountains
when the leaves fall from the trees.
Like how you can see inside a house
when the night falls and the lights turn on.
When you let your guard down
and show your inner self — your true self —
I can see true beauty in you.

At night, hold me tight.
I won't sleep.
At least, I'll find peace in your touch
and the steady rhythm of your heart.

I'm learning to tread in the deep waters of motherhood.

She has seen more pain in her short life,
than most of us will ever see.
And, yet, she chooses to see the best out of every day.

If we all used our pain to help others,
we would never feel alone.

Never apologize for standing up for yourself when no one else would.

Those hands,
that held me close
and held me tight,
are the same hands
that crushed me and
tore me away from all I knew.

I can't keep any of the good things
because, just like water can ruin stacks of pictures,
my tears have bled through all the good times.
Now the good and the bad memories stick together.
I can't tear them apart from each other
without damaging both.

You turned me inside out,
like a sweater,
exposing my seams,
my "handle with care,"
and the price of my sins.

I don't want to tell people how great they can be.
I want to show them how great they already are.

Make some light out of your dark.

You are not alone in your fight —
I
see
you.

Her neck was never designed to be your stress toy.

Find your truth and run with it.
See it through and discover who you really are.

I lost myself in the stars,
chasing after all the dreams
I've ever wished for.

Don't tell me you love me unless you really do.
I don't have enough time to waste
on explaining the difference.

You grow up fast when you find out something
you were never supposed to know about
too young.

She lives for today.
This, right now,
is all that matters.
She does not know
how much time she has left.

Take that leap,
even if it scares you.
You might find
you had all the tools already.

Find me broken in a garden of roses.
Search for me healing at the bottom of the ocean.

Go ahead and keep sharpening your knife
each time you think about me.
For it will become so sharp and shiny,
you won't be able to see me.
You'll fall in love with the reflection you see
and die at the blade meant for me.

The best way to remain unhappy is to remain the same.

She grieves for the sun, a best friend dying every night.

Be careful who you allow to see your vulnerable self. They may not know what to do with something so precious.

She uses her hands to create beautiful things,
while her mind destroys every good thing.

Dreams are snipers in the night,
they target our fears and our hopes,
destroying them as the sun rises.

The darkness seems to showcase our biggest struggles –
our demons on centre stage.
Our biggest fears in the spotlights —
their time to shine.

Don't wait for your chance to do something big,
look up and reach even further.

The sun only reflects how well we grow in the shade.

Identify it and then burn it.
Don't let your pain control your now.

Winter sun,
like seeing an old friend,
welcomed with open arms,
warming the soul on the coldest of days.

She needs the space to grow
and learn to become whole
without everyone else
trying to patch her up.

The enemy preys on the souls
of those who remain unclaimed —
using them until they are nothing but dust.

Pry her open.
Burn her exterior.
Force her out.
She's still in there,
no matter what she's survived.

The blaze has burnt the walls of my house.
I hold the key to escape,
but I'm mesmerized by the smoke.

I'm getting more comfortable spending time alone.
Finally, enjoying my own company.

When I see mountains, I see challenges.
When the rain falls, I see growth.

The giants who stood over her never scared her,
for she saw her own courage as bigger than theirs.

I've learned to love the pain that has made me who I am.
I've learned to kiss the scars that have kept me alive.

She has a soul so entangled in heaven,
she cannot be harmed by earthly things.

I'm still not sure how you got in.
I had locked every door to my heart —
barricaded every window.
Still, you found me there.

Her deep roots
remind her she has a home.
Her seeds run free with the wind —
allowing her dreams
to find new ground to grow.

Pour water onto my scars
and I hope it kills the fire that made them.

She doesn't feel the need to cover her scars
because she's learned to love them.

Love me or hate me.
It doesn't really make a difference.
It's never been about how you see me.
It's about how I see myself.

Whoever said "depression is all in your head"
has never felt the physical pain of it.
Sharp muscle pain in the shoulders and neck from the
weight of the negative thoughts.
Stomach cramping, holding all that worry inside.
Migraines from fighting for my soul all day and night.
They have never noticed the exhaustion in my bones.
I'll have to battle through the night,
just to go to war once more in the morning.
Depression is heavy.
It's ruthless.
It never gives up.
But,
neither do I.

I'm the closest to her,
the one who knows her best,
that's why I'm the easiest one to hurt.

I'm tired of fighting.
My armour feels heavy,
my skin and spirit are bruised.
My heart has been stitched back together,
but is barely holding on.
My head is cracked like a broken porcelain doll;
fragile.
I'm limping with every step;
a wounded soldier.
I'm broken and bleeding,
but it's all invisible.
My pain and my scars hidden,
the me you see is nothing but lies,
behind nice clothes, curled hair, make-up and a smile.

She loves getting lost in the woods to remember who she is.

I have a sickness –
a darkness inside of me.
You have it too.
I can see it in the claw marks and the bites on you.
You're covered in white scars where it tried to burn you.
The worst pain you've kept hidden under your skin.

I've smiled that smile.
A warrior knee deep in the trenches of your mind;
a survivor of hard times;
a fighter of the unseen.
An ember trying to ignite a fire
to burn all the darkness away,
so that all is left is a blaze of light.

I'm trying.
I'm trying so hard!
The waves,
those same waves that I called here to change things,
have destroyed everything I had built.

It's a lonely thing
to be up all day and all night
with no one to talk to but myself.

Loud thoughts circle
round and round.
They roar out loud.
In cries of wolves,
gathering likeminded spirits,
growing an army against those who
made my mind go wild.

Her laugh puts a smile in everyone's heart.

I tell you my secrets.
You use them against me.
Ask me why I don't trust you.

This cycle will end with me.

She is a queen and she doesn't need to explain herself to anyone.

It's a lonely life
when you play
only your own music
through the speakers.

You care more how strangers view you
than staying loyal to those who love you.
You would throw me to the wolves
without a second thought
if it meant getting someone else's approval.

Finding peace in the brokenness
is the only way you can rebuild.

I submerged myself underwater,
made sure every inch of my body was covered.
I will never be dry enough
to let myself become consumed by that flame.
Never again.

If the leaves have the courage
to grow back every year,
after they've tried every colour
only to fall and freeze,
so will I.

Look at it all.
All that poison swimming in her veins.
She can't escape it
but she tries.

Sometimes,
my mascara smears across my cheeks.
Other times,
a thinly spooled spider web
traps me.
You can only see it in the right light.
Pain.

She didn't want to settle for a cage when the sky was calling.

She laughs with abandon never fearing the thief of joy.

Sometimes I like when I'm covered in scratches and
bruises.
At least, then, other people see that I'm hurt
and that I, too, can bleed.

She becomes unstoppable when she learns,
she doesn't need wings to fly.

I rely on these legs to walk me through life,
but I never thought they'd be so still
when I needed to run away from *him*.

I project all my fears out into the world
and then wonder why
it's so scary to live in it.

Hold me tight.
Let's wait for the waves to stop crashing over us,
before we drop anchor
and build our house here
in the middle of this dark ocean.

It hurts to want.
It's hard to feel so much
but never quite reach it.

She makes me brave as much as she makes me weak.

Finding peace in the chaos.
Finding serenity in the mess.
It can wait,
I am healing.
You can't blame the dirt that's settled here.
I've been working on myself.
Some other things will fall apart,
be put aside.
They can wait,
I am healing.
I don't need to apologize
for putting myself first.
Everything can wait
until I am me again.

She sees everyday as a new adventure to discover herself.

She never allows anyone to tell her how to think,
but shows them what she knows.
She's capable of more than they give her credit for.

An escape to the mind helps to escape the passage of time.

I hope that, when I'm gone,
she will look at my life and see
that everything I ever did
was all for her.

I'm a trapped bird,
sedated by my own mind.
The cage is open
but I'm too tired to fly.

We are all connected.
We need to treat everything better,
starting with ourselves.

She held onto too much
and now her life is full of chaos.

He said I was beautiful when I was sad,
maybe that's why he always made me cry.

I don't want to hide under a rock.
I want to take the seeds of pain,
bury them deep into the ground.
Water them and watch them grow into
a big garden filled with beautiful flowers.

My mind has a rusty gate and a cheap lock.
It doesn't take much work for evil thoughts
to come storming in and destroying
the beautiful garden that's growing
within.

Behind the dark clouds full of rain,
I was healing through the pain.
The ghosts have haunted my best efforts.
New growth stomped over,
so that I must begin again —
reseed my scars again,
bring back the rain,
for flowers to grow there again.

ABOUT THE AUTHOR

Michelle Young lives in Ottawa, Canada with her husband and daughter. Struggling with depression, infertility, and trauma from a past abusive relationship, Michelle wants to help others by sharing her story and inviting readers along her healing journey.

If you enjoyed this book, please make sure to leave a review and follow Michelle Young on Facebook, Instagram and Goodreads.

Facebook.com/michelleyoungauthor
Instagram @michelleyoungauthor
www.michelleyoungauthor.com

www.ingramcontent.com/pod-product-compliance
Lightning Source LLC
Chambersburg PA
CBHW060012050426
42448CB00012B/2721